Simple, Tasty, Good

Plant-based recipes for top taste and vital health

Simple, Tasty, Good

Plant-based recipes for top taste and vital health

Proudly published and printed in Australia.

This book was
Edited by Nathan Brown
Proofread by Talitha Simmons
Designed by DEC Creatives
Food photography by Gary and Dyanne Dixon of Dixon Photography
Cover design by DEC Creatives
Typeset in Helvetica Neue

Simply Enjoy the Optimal Diet

We believe good health should be simple.

Dr Colin Campbell summarizes a lifetime of health research health by saying, "One of the most fortunate findings from the mountain of nutritional research I have encountered is that good food and good health is simple. . . . The recommendations coming from the published literature are so simple that I can state them in one sentence: eat a whole foods, plant-based diet, while minimising the consumption of refined food, added salt and added fats."*

During the past three years, the Choose Life team have been responsible for supervising more than 50 Coronary Health Improvement Project (CHIP) seminars, where the simple principles of a whole-food plant-based diet, exercise, adequate water intake and trust have enabled hundreds of people to dramatically improve their health. The CHIP Seminar has been compiled by Dr Hans Diehl, researcher and clinical professor of preventive medicine at Loma Linda University California, USA. From his research, Dr Diehl has pulled together the simple nutritional principles into the "Optimal Diet."

Participants from this program have repeatedly asked us for a recipe book they can use for implementing the principles of the Optimal Diet in their homes. This book is a response to those requests.

Each recipe in this book had to meet three criteria:
1. The recipes had to taste good;
2. The ingredients had to be readily available in supermarkets; and
3. They had to be good for you.

The Optimal Diet is a comprehensive way of analyzing and finding ways to improve your diet so you can live a happier and healthier life with the ones you love.

So before you get into exploring some of the healthy and delicious recipes we have collected in this book, here are some general principles on which these recipes have been based:

Eat more

Hearty Breakfasts Enjoy hot, multigrain cereals, fresh fruit and whole-wheat toast. Make breakfast a big deal and jump-start your day.

Whole Grains Freely use brown rice, millet, barley, corn, wheat and rye. Also eat freely of wholegrain products, such as breads, pastas, shredded wheat and tortillas.

Tubers and Legumes Freely use all varieties of white potatoes, sweet potatoes and yams (without high-fat toppings). Enjoy peas, lentils, chickpeas and beans of every kind.

Water Drink six to eight glasses of water a day. Vary the routine with a twist of lemon or use herbal teas.

Fruits and Vegetables Eat several fresh, whole fruits every day. Limit fruits canned in syrup and fibre-poor fruit juices. Eat a variety of vegetables daily. Enjoy fresh salads with low-calorie, low-salt dressings.

Eat less

Visible Fats and Oils Avoid fatty meats. Strictly limit cooking and salad oils, sauces, dressings and shortening. Use margarine and nuts only sparingly. Avoid frying— saute instead with a little water in non-stick pans.

Sugars Limit sugar, honey, molasses, syrups, pies, cakes, pastries, cookies, soda drinks and sugar-rich desserts, like ice-cream. Save these foods for special occasions.

High-cholesterol Foods Avoid meat, sausages, egg yolks and liver. Limit dairy products, if used, to low-fat cheeses and non-fat milk products. If you eat fish and poultry, use only sparingly.

Salt Use minimal salt during cooking. Strictly limit highly-salted products like pickles, crackers, soy sauce, salted popcorn, nuts, chips, pretzels and garlic salt.

Alcohol Avoid alcohol in all forms, as well as caffeinated beverages such as coffee, colas and black tea.

The Optimal Diet recommends that the total amount of fat consumed in your diet should account for less than 20 per cent of the total energy (calories) consumed. In order to enable you to make intelligent decisions about what you are going to cook, we have included a nutritional analysis for each recipe. This nutritional analysis includes the percentage of energy from fats, carbohydrates and proteins for each recipe. Optional ingredients have not been included in the nutritional analysis.

Because these recipes are all plant-based, none of the recipes contain cholesterol.

This recipe book is filled with fantastic new recipes, based on the guidelines given by the Optimal Diet. These recipes taste great, are quick and easy to make, and—to top it off—they are good for you!

Enjoy food with friends and family, and create a lifetime of memories. Choose life!

The "Choose Life!" team
Auckland, New Zealand

*T Colin Campbell and Thomas M Campbell, The China Study, Benbella Books, Dallas, 2006, page 242.

Contents

Hearty soups

Apricot, Beet and Cumin Soup

6 medium beets, peeled and
chopped
1 tbsp lime juice
¾ cup dried apricots,
chopped
2 red onions, chopped
1 clove garlic, crushed
1 tsp cumin
1 tsp paprika
5 cups low-salt vegetable
stock
2½ cups orange juice
salt and pepper to taste
coriander to garnish

1 Place beets, lime juice, apricots, onions, garlic, cumin, paprika and vegetable stock in a large saucepan. Bring to the boil, then cover and simmer gently for 45 minutes. Transfer mixture to a food processor and blend until smooth. (Soup can be frozen at this point for later use.)

2 Add orange juice, and season to taste with salt and pepper.

3 Garnish with chopped coriander.

PER SERVE: *Energy 514 kJ (123 Cal); Protein 3g (10%); Carbohydrates 24g (86%); Sugars 22g; Fat 1g (4%); Fibre 3g; Sodium 387mg; Calcium 30mg.*

SERVES 8

Brown Lentil and Tomato Soup

½–¾ cup brown lentils

1 tsp oil

1 large onion, chopped

1 large carrot, coarsely grated

2 sticks of celery, finely chopped

4 cups low-salt vegetable stock

15oz can crushed tomatoes

15oz can concentrated low-salt tomato soup

1 tsp garlic powder or 1 clove of garlic, crushed

1 tbsp Italian herbs or fresh herbs of choice

salt to taste (optional)

1 Saute onions, carrot and celery lightly in oil, with a small amount of water. When onion is clear, add lentils, stock and crushed tomatoes, and simmer until lentils are cooked (approximately 30 minutes).

2 Add tomato soup, garlic and herbs. Simmer for a few more minutes. Season to taste.

PER SERVE: *Energy 353 kJ (84 Cal); Protein 3g (13%); Carbohydrates 15g (75%); Sugars 10g (12%); Fat 1g; Fibre 3g; Sodium 712mg; Calcium 40mg.*

SERVES 8

Pasta and Bean Soup

1 large clove garlic,
finely chopped
1 medium onion, finely
chopped
1 tbsp water
2 bay leaves
1 tsp basil
15oz can Italian tomatoes
15oz can mixed beans
4 cups vegetable stock
1 cup pasta shells
salt and pepper to taste
(optional)

1 Heat water in a large saucepan, then add garlic and onion. Cook without browning until the onion is soft and clear. Stir in bay leaves and basil, and cook for a minute longer.

2 Add tomatoes, mixed beans and stock. Bring to the boil and add pasta. Simmer, stirring occasionally, until the pasta is tender (10–15 minutes). Season to taste. Remove bay leaves before serving.

PER SERVE: *Energy 1334 kJ (321 Cal); Protein 13g (16%); Carbohydrates 60g (80%); Sugars 7g; Fat 1g (4%); Fibre 8g; Sodium 635mg; Calcium 70mg.*

SERVES 6

Potato and Leek Soup

6–8 large potatoes, peeled and
diced
3 leeks (or more)
1 tbsp olive oil
2 stock cubes
5 cups boiling water
½ tsp thyme
pinch of pepper
2 tbsp chopped parsley

1 Heat oil in a large saucepan and saute leeks until soft. Add remaining ingredients, except parsley. Simmer for 30 minutes or until soft.

2 Blend in food processor or blender when cool. Reheat to serve and garnish with parsley.

PER SERVE: *Energy 865 kJ (207 Cal); Protein 7g (14%); Carbohydrates 35g (74%); Sugars 3g; Fat 3g (12%); Fibre 6g; Sodium 273mg; Calcium 33mg.*

SERVES 6

Pumpkin and Kumara Soup

1 tbsp oil
2 small onions, chopped
2 cloves garlic, crushed
1¼lb pumpkin
2 medium kumara (sweet potatoes)
4 cups low-salt vegetable stock
1 tsp orange zest
2 tbsp orange juice
salt and pepper to taste
4–6 chives, finely chopped (optional)

1 Heat oil in a large saucepan. Add onion and garlic, stirring until onion softens and goes clear.

2 Add peeled and chopped pumpkin, kumara and stock, and bring to boil. Reduce heat and simmer covered for about 15 minutes, or until pumpkin and kumara are tender. Cool for 10 minutes.

3 Blend or process pumpkin mixture until smooth. Return smooth mixture to pan. Add zest and juice.

Stir over heat, without boiling, until heated through. Season to taste and serve topped with chives.

PER SERVE: *Energy 845 kJ (202 Cal); Protein 5g (10%); Carbohydrates 34g (70%); Sugars 14g; Fat 4g (20%); Fibre 4g; Sodium 571mg; Calcium 70mg.*

SERVES 4

Vegetable and Red Lentil Soup

1 large onion, chopped
2 cloves garlic, chopped
1 tsp oil
2 stalks celery, chopped
2 large carrots, chopped
4 cups pumpkin or squash, cut into chunks
½ tsp curry powder
2½ tsp paprika
¼ tsp nutmeg
1 cup red lentils
4 cups vegetable stock
15oz can low-salt tomato soup concentrate

1 Heat oil in a large pan. Add onion, garlic and a small amount of water. Saute until onion softens.
2 Add vegetables, then stir for another minute. Add spices, lentils and vegetable stock. Simmer until vegetables are tender, for approximately 20 minutes.

3 Blend or food process soup and add tomato soup. Thin with water to desired conistency.

PER SERVE: *Energy 948 kJ (227 Cal); Protein 11g (20%); Carbohydrates 36g (71%); Sugars 15g; Fat 2g (9%); Fibre 8g; Sodium 632mg; Calcium 66mg.*

SERVES 8

Spicy Dhal Soup

¾ cup red lentils
4 cups water
1½ tbsp mustard seeds
1 onion, diced
1 large carrot
1 large potato, cubed
3 cloves garlic, crushed
1 tsp cumin
1 tsp turmeric
½ tsp salt
1–3 tsp grated ginger
15oz can chopped tomatoes

1 Wash lentils until water runs clear. Drain in a sieve. Place the lentils in 2 cups of water in a large saucepan. Simmer gently, stirring often, for 15 minutes or until the lentils are soft and mushy.
2 Heat a little water in another saucepan over a medium heat. Cook mustard seeds while stirring, until the seeds begin to pop. Add onion and cook until transparent. Add remaining water and all other ingredients. Simmer while stirring occasionally, until vegetables are tender (about 20–30 minutes).

PER SERVE: *Energy 406 kJ (97 Cal); Protein 4g (17%); Carbohydrates 13g (63%); Sugars 5g; Fat 2g (20%); Fibre 4g; Sodium 337mg; Calcium 50mg.*

SERVES 6

Main meals

Asparagus Pasta

1 or 2 bunches thin asparagus
spears
13oz dry pasta
juice of 1 lemon
⅓ cup water
1 tbsp oil
3 large cloves of garlic,
crushed
1 tbsp sweet chilli sauce
½ cup baby spinach
2 tbsp basil
freshly ground black pepper
salt to taste
spray cooking oil

1 Break off woody ends of asparagus spears. Spray spears with oil, and grill until tender and slightly charred. Remove from grill and cut into bite-sized pieces. Toss in a bowl with half lemon juice.

2 Cook pasta according to the packet and drain.

3 While pasta is cooking, combine oil with garlic and sweet chilli sauce in a large, non-stick frying pan. Cook over low heat until garlic is fragrant for about 5 minutes. Add water and remaining lemon juice, and bring to the boil. Add grilled asparagus and drained pasta, and toss over the heat.

4 Transfer to a bowl. Add basil and spinach, and toss again. Season with salt and pepper, if desired. Serve immediately.

PER SERVE: *Energy 1552 kJ (371 Cal); Protein 12g (13%); Carbohydrates 67g (76%); Sugars 3g; Fat 5g (11%); Fibre 5g; Sodium 40mg; Calcium 35mg.*

SERVES 4

German Pasta Bake

Sauce:

½ cup raw cashews
1 cup non-dairy milk
1 tbsp plain flour
1½ stock cubes
1 tsp savory yeast flakes
1 tsp onion powder or
½ onion
¼ tsp celery salt
½ cup soft tofu
1 tbsp lemon juice
1½ cups water

Pasta:

2 cups dry macaroni
1 cup regular tofu, mashed
⅓ cup parsley
6 spring onions, chopped
½ tsp dill
1 tsp mixed herbs
1 cup fresh breadcrumbs

Sauce:

1 Chop cashews in food processor or blender until powdery.

2 Add other sauce ingredients and process until smooth.

Pasta:

1 Cook macaroni according to instructions on the packet.

2 Combine tofu, herbs, spring onions and pasta in a casserole dish. Pour sauce evenly over pasta mixture.

3 Cover and bake for 30 minutes at 350°F.

4 Uncover, sprinkle breadcrumbs over the top and cook for a further 15 minutes.

PER SERVE: *Energy 844 kJ (202 Cal); Protein 10g (20%); Carbohydrates 20g (43%); Sugars 3g; Fat 8g (37%); Fibre 3g; Sodium 290mg; Calcium 114mg.*

SERVES 8

Lasagna

Sauce:
1 medium onion, chopped
½ tsp oil
1 tbsp dried basil
1 carrot, grated
1 zucchini, grated
15oz cooked brown lentils
15oz can chopped tomatoes
5oz tin tomato paste
¼ tsp salt

½ packet instant lasagna sheets

White sauce:
½ cup cashews
1 tbsp all-purpose flour
2 cups water
1 small red bell pepper
1 tsp salt
½ small onion
1 clove garlic

Sauce:
1 Saute onion until soft. Add basil and cook for another minute.

2 Add carrot, zucchini, brown lentils, tomatoes, tomato paste and salt. Bring mixture to the boil, then reduce heat and simmer for 5 minutes.

White sauce:
1 Blend all ingredients in food processor or blender until smooth, then place in a saucepan and bring to the boil. Boil until thick.

To assemble lasagna:
1 Place a small amount of sauce in the base of a baking dish.

2 Cover with one layer of lasagna sheets, then spread half the remaining sauce over the top. Cover with lasagna sheets.

3 Continue layering until all the tomato sauce is used, finishing with a layer of lasagna sheets. Cover the last layer of lasagna sheets with the white sauce.

PER SERVE: *Energy 985 kJ (235 Cal); Protein 9g (15%); Carbohydrates 26g (49%); Sugars 6g; Fat 10g (36%); Fibre 6g; Sodium 676mg; Calcium 58mg.*

SERVES 6–8

Sundried Tomato and Spinach Pasta

13oz uncooked penne pasta
3 small spring onions,
finely chopped
9 sundried tomatoes, cut into
thin strips
2 cups baby spinach
2–3 tbsp pine nuts or
chopped cashews toasted
(optional)
fresh oregano or herb of
choice to taste

Dressing:
1 tsp oil
3 tbsp water
1–2 tbsp lemon juice
2 medium cloves garlic,
crushed
1–2 tbsp sweet chilli sauce
salt to taste (optional)

1 Cook pasta according to packet instructions until tender. Drain and rinse under lukewarm water.

2 Transfer to large bowl. Add spring onions, tomatoes, spinach, pine nuts and oregano to pasta and toss.

3 Mix dressing ingredients and pour over pasta. Toss well and serve.

4 Garnish with nuts, oregano and sundried tomatoes.

PER SERVE: *Energy 1079 kJ (258 Cal); Protein 9g (14%); Carbohydrates 49g (79%); Sugars 6g; Fat 2g (7%); Fibre 4g; Sodium 57mg; Calcium 31mg.*

SERVES 6

Italian Tofu Balls

12oz firm tofu, mashed
1 clove garlic, finely chopped
1 onion, finely chopped
¼ cup pecan nuts, chopped
2 slices whole wheat bread, crumbed
1 tbsp all-purpose flour (to bind)
2 tsp low-salt soya sauce
2 tbsp freshly cut parsley or chives
½ tsp sweet basil
¼ tsp salt

Tomato sauce:
2 tsp olive oil (optional)
¼ tsp sweet basil
1 onion, chopped
¼ tsp crushed garlic
15oz can tomato puree or soup
1 tsp sugar
¼ tsp salt

1 Preheat oven to 350°F. Combine tofu-ball ingredients in a bowl and mix thoroughly.

2 Form mixture into 16 balls. Place on an oiled non-stick baking tray.

3 Bake for 30–40 minutes, turning halfway through cooking time.

Sauce:

1 Heat oil in pan, and saute onion and garlic until soft.

2 Stir in tomato puree, sugar, basil and salt.

3 Drop tofu balls in sauce—don't stir, just cover.

3 Serve hot with cooked spaghetti.

PER SERVE: *Energy 618 kJ (147 Cal); Protein 8g (21%); Carbohydrates 11g (38%); Sugars 6g; Fat 7g (41%); Fibre 4g; Sodium 544mg; Calcium 91mg.*

SERVES 4–6

Roasted Vegetable Pasta

1¾lb various root vegetables
(potato, kumara
(sweet potato), etc)
spray cooking oil
8oz pasta
1 small head of broccoli
¼ cup toasted cashews or
pine nuts (optional)
2 tbsp lemon juice
1 tbsp olive oil
2–3 tbsp basil
salt and black pepper
(optional)

1 Preheat oven to 400°F. Chop root vegetables into 1-inch cubes. Place on a baking tray and spray with oil. Roast for 20 minutes or until vegetables are cooked.

2 While vegetables are cooking, cut broccoli into small florets. Cook pasta according to the instructions on the packet. In the last few minutes, add broccoli and bring back to the boil.

3 Combine drained pasta, broccoli, roasted vegetables and nuts.

4 Mix basil with lemon juice and oil, and drizzle over pasta. Season to taste and serve.

PER SERVE: *Energy 1762 kJ (420 Cal); Protein 13g (13%); Carbohydrates 77g (77%); Sugars 7g; Fat 5g (10%); Fibre 8g; Sodium 36mg; Calcium 127mg.*

SERVES 4

Vegetables and Pasta with Satay Sauce

8–10oz whole wheat pasta or
noodles
1 medium or large carrot, cut
into matchsticks
1 medium zucchini, halved
and sliced diagonally
7oz broccoli, cut into small
florets, or green beans, sliced

Dressing:
½ cup peanut butter
½ cup hot water
2 tbsp low-salt soy sauce
2 tbsp lemon juice
1 tbsp brown sugar
1 tsp minced ginger
salt or garlic salt to taste
(optional)
1 tbsp sweet chilli sauce

1 Cook pasta according to instructions on the packet. When
pasta is almost cooked, add the
vegetables to the saucepan. Cook
for 1–2 minutes longer until vegetables are just cooked.

2 Combine dressing ingredients
and mix to break up peanut butter.

3 Drain the vegetables and pasta
well. Return to the saucepan, add
the dressing and toss gently until
well combined.

4 Serve garnished with chopped
spring onions.

PER SERVE: *Energy 2185 kJ (522 Cal);
Protein 22g (17%); Carbohydrates 57g
(48%); Sugars 8g; Fat 21g (35%); Fibre
9g; Sodium 418mg; Calcium 65mg.*

SERVES 4

Roasted Vegetables

potato
pumpkin
kumara (sweet potato)
parsnip
zucchini
portabella mushrooms
onion
garlic
salt
spray cooking oil

1 Use any amount of seasonal vegetables. Scrub or thinly peel kumara (sweet potato), pumpkin, potatoes, parsnip and more, and cut into even slices ½ inch thick. Cut unpeeled zucchini in ½-inch diagonal slices. Trim large portabella mushrooms. Peel and cut onion into wedges. Add garlic.

2 Spray vegetables with oil. Cook on a double-sided grill for 10–15 minutes, or roast at 400°F in a baking dish for 20–30 minutes, turning halfway through. Cook until golden brown and tender.

PER SERVE: *Energy 895 kJ (214 Cal); Protein 5g (9%); Carbohydrates 22g (46%); Sugars 6g; Fat 11g (45%); Fibre 6g; Sodium 171mg; Calcium 44mg.*

SERVES 4

Capsicum and Avocado Salsa

5oz sweet corn kernels
½ red bell pepper (capsicum), diced
1 spring onion, sliced
juice of 1 lemon
1 small avocado, peeled and chopped

1 Mix all ingredients in a small bowl and serve over baked potatoes, nachos or tacos.

PER SERVE: *Energy 348 kJ (83 Cal); Protein 1g (6%); Carbohydrates 4g (20%); Sugars 1g; Fat 7g (74%); Fibre 1g; Sodium 43mg; Calcium 10mg.*

SERVES 8

Baked Potatoes with Lentil Sauce

6 medium potatoes, washed
1 onion, chopped
1 carrot, grated
1 tsp oil
½ tsp curry (optional)
15oz cooked brown lentils
13oz low-salt tomato pasta sauce

1 Prick the skin of the potatoes several times. Place on paper towel around the edge of microwave turntable. Cook potatoes uncovered on high for about 12 minutes or until potatoes are tender. Or bake the potatoes in a hot oven 400°F for about an hour.

2 Saute onion and carrot in oil, with a small amount of water, until the onion is soft. Add lentils and pasta sauce. Heat through.

3 Cut a cross in the top of the cooked potato and gently push open. Spoon topping into and over baked potato.

Variation: Serve with Capsicum and Avocado Salsa (as pictured).

PER SERVE: *Energy 788 kJ (188 Cal); Protein 8g (17%); Carbohydrates 31g (73%); Sugars 4g; Fat 2g (10%); Fibre 7g; Sodium 248mg; Calcium 34mg.*

SERVES 6

Tuscany Potatoes

6lb potatoes
2 tsp turmeric
spray cooking oil

***Topping*:**
1 onion, chopped
2 cloves of garlic, crushed
1 red bell pepper, chopped
½ tsp oil
2 x 15oz cans chopped
tomatoes
15oz can chickpeas, drained
and rinsed
½ tsp salt
parsley, chopped
lemon juice (to serve)

1 Preheat oven to 350°F. Slice unpeeled potatoes into ½-inch thick slices.

2 Coat with turmeric and spray oil, and place in roasting dish. Roast for about 1 hour until potatoes are cooked (turn at least once).

3 Place onion, bell pepper and garlic in a large cooking pot with oil. Cook for about 5 minutes until clear. Add tomatoes and chick-peas, and mash. Season to taste.

4 Place potatoes on a platter and squeeze lemon juice over them. Cover potatoes with tomato top-ping mixture. Garnish with parsley.

PER SERVE: *Energy 1941 kJ (464 Cal); Protein 18g (16%); Carbohydrates 82g (79%); Sugars 9g; Fat 3g (5%); Fibre 16g; Sodium 474mg; Calcium 97mg.*

SERVES 6

Shepherd's Pie

Base:

2 medium onions, finely chopped
4 cloves of garlic, finely chopped
1 tbsp oil
2 cups brown lentils, washed
4 cups water
2 x 15oz cans chopped tomatoes
3 tsp Italian herbs
2 tbsp tomato paste
2 tsp oregano
salt to taste (optional)

Topping:

2 large kumara (sweet potatoes), peeled and cubed
¼ regular pumpkin or squash, peeled and cubed
non-dairy milk
salt to taste (optional)

Base:

1 Put half of one onion aside. Cook remaining onion and garlic in a large saucepan with oil until translucent.

2 Add water and brown lentils, then cook for 20–30 minutes or until lentils are soft. Add the rest of the base ingredients and stir.

Topping:

1 Boil kumara and pumpkin for 10–20 minutes or until the kumara and pumpkin are soft. Drain and roughly mash, adding chopped half onion. Add enough non-dairy milk to make a desired consistency and season to taste.

2 Preheat oven to 400°F. In a casserole dish, pour the lentil mixture into the bottom and cover with the mashed topping.

3 Bake for 10 minutes or until crisp around the edges.

PER SERVE: *Energy 1069 kJ (255 Cal); Protein 17g (27%); Carbohydrates 32g (60%); Sugars 7g; Fat 4g (13%); Fibre 12g; Sodium 131mg; Calcium 109mg.*

SERVES 6

Brown Rice Pilaf

3 small kumara (sweet
potatoes), chopped into
½-inch cubes
cooking oil spray
4½ cups low-salt vegetable
stock
2 tsp oil
2 brown onions,
finely chopped
3 cloves garlic, crushed
2 trimmed celery stalks,
finely chopped
7oz mushrooms,
coarsely chopped
2¼ cups brown
medium-grain rice
2–3 tbsp lemon rind
pepper to taste
¾ cup loosely-packed
parsley leaves

1 Preheat oven to 350°F. Place kumara on lightly-oiled oven tray. Spray with oil and roast uncovered for 20–30 minutes until tender.

2 Bring stock to boil in medium saucepan, reduce heat and simmer uncovered for 10 minutes.

3 Heat oil in medium saucepan. Cook onion, garlic and celery, stirring until onion softens. Add mushrooms and rice, and cook for 2 minutes. Add stock and reduce heat. Simmer covered for 50 minutes or until stock is absorbed and rice is tender. Add more stock if necessary. Gently stir in kumara, rind and parsley. Serve topped with parsley.

PER SERVE: *Energy 2583 kJ (617 Cal); Protein 14g (9%); Carbohydrates 122g (83%); Sugars 11g; Fat 6g (8%); Fibre 10g; Sodium 683mg; Calcium 87mg.*

SERVES 4

Thai Risotto

1 piece lemon grass, finely chopped
2 small lemons or regular limes, remove and retain zest
1½ cups brown or basmati rice
1 tbsp oil
1 large onion, finely chopped
1 inch fresh root ginger, peeled and finely chopped
1½ coriander seeds
1½ tsp cumin seeds
3 cups low-salt vegetable stock
4 tbsp chopped fresh coriander
lemon or lime wedges to serve (optional)

1 Rinse rice under cold water and drain through sieve. Heat oil in a large saucepan and add onion, spices, lemon grass and lemon zest. Cook gently for 2–3 minutes.

2 Add rice and cook for a further minute, then add stock and bring to the boil. Reduce heat to very low and cover the pan.

3 Cook gently for 30 minutes—stirring occasionally—then check the rice. If it is still crunchy, cover the pan and leave for a further 3–5 minutes until the rice is tender.

4 Stir in the fresh coriander. Stir with a fork to separate the grains and leave for 10 minutes. Serve with lemon or lime wedges.

PER SERVE: *Energy 1476 kJ (353 Cal); Protein 7g (9%); Carbohydrates 66g (77%); Sugars 6g; Fat 6g (14%); Fibre 4g; Sodium 425mg; Calcium 42mg.*

SERVES 4

Chickpea Korma

1 tbsp oil
2 onions, finely chopped
2 tbsp ginger, chopped
2 tsp mustard seeds
2 tsp cumin
2 tsp coriander
2 tsp curry powder
2 x 15oz cans low-salt
chopped tomatoes
¼ –½ x 15oz can lite coconut
cream
½ tsp salt
10oz spinach, fresh or frozen,
chopped
2 x 15oz cans chickpeas,
drained and rinsed
2 tbsp fresh coriander or
parsley

1 Saute onion until translucent. Add ginger and spices, and cook for 2 minutes. Add tomatoes and simmer for 10 minutes, allowing flavors to mingle. Add remaining ingredients.

2 Serve on rice. Garnish with coriander or parsley.

3 If cooking in advance, cook everything except coconut cream, chickpeas and spinach, and store in fridge.

PER SERVE: *Energy 1171 kJ (280 Cal); Protein 13g (18%); Carbohydrates 27g (48%); Sugars 8g; Fat 11g (34%); Fibre 10g; Sodium 657mg; Calcium 147mg.*

SERVES 6

Indian Chickpeas

1 onion, finely chopped
2 tbsp water
1 tsp curry powder
1 tsp garam masala
½ tsp ground ginger
½ tsp cumin
15oz can tomato puree
15oz can Indian tomatoes
¾ cup lite coconut milk or
non-dairy milk
15oz can chickpeas, drained
2 medium boiled potatoes,
cubed
1½ cup cauliflower, cut into
florets
1 cup frozen peas
chopped coriander or parsley
(to garnish)
½ tsp salt (optional)

1 Saute onion with water in a large pan, stirring frequently, until the onion is clear. Mix in curry powder, garam masala, ginger and cumin. Continue to cook, stirring frequently, for 1–2 minutes longer.

2 Add tomato puree, tomatoes, coconut milk, chickpeas, potatoes, cauliflower and peas. Simmer for about 5 minutes until cauliflower is just tender.

3 Season to taste. Use chopped coriander or parsley to garnish.

4 Serve over steamed basmati rice or brown rice with roti.

PER SERVE: *Energy 1018 kJ (243 Cal); Protein 10g (17%); Carbohydrates 27g (52%); Sugars 10g; Fat 9g (31%); Fibre 10g; Sodium 481mg; Calcium 80mg.*

SERVES 6

Spicy Fesenjan

1 onion, chopped
1–2 tsp curry powder
½ tsp allspice
½ tsp cinnamon
½ tsp ginger
½ tsp nutmeg
2 tsp oil or cooking oil spray
½ x 15oz can tomato puree
15oz can chickpeas, reserve liquid
½ cup liquid from chickpeas
¼ cup roasted peanuts, chopped

1 Heat oil in a saucepan, then saute the spices for 2 minutes. Add onions and saute. Cook until very soft (almost mushy) and clear. Add a little of the chickpea liquid if the onions become too dry.

2 Add tomato puree and chickpea liquid, and stir well. Simmer for 5 minutes. Add chickpeas and peanuts, and simmer for 15 minutes. Add more liquid if mixture is too dry. Mixture should be thick but not sloppy.

3 Serve with couscous or rice.

PER SERVE: *Energy 1171 kJ (280 Cal); Protein 13g (19%); Carbohydrates 22g (37%); Sugars 5g; Fat 14g (44%); Fibre 8g; Sodium 534mg; Calcium 83mg.*

SERVES 4

Roti (Indian flat bread)

½ cup white flour
½ cup whole wheat flour
boiling water

1 Mix flours. Add enough boiling water to make a soft dough. Gently knead for a couple of minutes until smooth. Divide dough into 8 pieces. Roll each piece out into a flat circle.

2 Cook in a dry non-stick frying pan over medium heat for a minute or two, turning when bread gets a few brown spots on the underside. Cook until other side gets a few brown spots. The bread will have patches that will rise with air bubbles during cooking.

3 Put on plate and cover with clean tea towel until all breads are cooked. Serve with curry, dahl or other fillings.

PER SERVE: *Energy 508 kJ (121 Cal); Protein 4g (13%); Carbohydrates 23g (83%); Sugars 0g; Fat 1g (4%); Fibre 3g; Sodium 1mg; Calcium 9mg.*

SERVES 4

Thai-style Curry

1 carrot, cut into matchsticks
1 red bell pepper, cut into matchsticks
1 green bell pepper, cut into matchsticks
4 zucchinis, cut into matchsticks
1 onion, cut into matchsticks
2 cloves garlic, crushed
1 cup tomato puree
1 tbsp low-salt soya sauce
1 cup cooked chickpeas or lentils
2 tbsp peanut butter
1 tbsp curry powder
1 cup frozen beans

1 Place carrot, onion, bell pepper, garlic and curry powder in a saucepan with a small amount of water. Simmer for about 5 minutes until tender. Add zucchini, cover and simmer 5 minutes more.

2 Blend peanut butter, soya sauce and tomato puree until smooth. Add to cooked vegetables with chickpeas or lentils and frozen beans. Heat until beans are cooked.

3 Serve over rice.

PER SERVE: *Energy 1013 kJ (242 Cal); Protein 13g (22%); Carbohydrates 25g (51%); Sugars 12g; Fat 7g (27%); Fibre 12g; Sodium 599mg; Calcium 119mg.*

SERVES 4

Potato Samosas

2 medium potatoes, cooked and cubed
1 medium onion, finely diced
1 clove garlic
1 tbsp oil
1 tsp curry powder
1 tsp ground cumin
½ tsp turmeric
½ cup frozen mixed vegetables or peas
2 tbsp water
½ tsp salt
juice of half a lemon
2–3 tbsp fresh coriander (optional)
12 sheets filo pastry
spray cooking oil

1 Cook onion and garlic in a large pan with oil until the onion is soft. Add curry powder, cumin and turmeric, and cook for another 2 minutes.

2 Add mixed vegetables and water, then cover and cook for a few minutes. Stir in potato, salt, lemon juice and coriander. Taste and adjust seasonings if necessary.

3 Layer three sheets of filo, brushing between the layers with a small amount of oil. Cut the filo into 4 strips crossways.

4 Place a spoonful of the filling at the top of each filo strip. Fold the filo over so the top touches the edge, forming a triangle. Keep folding in triangles to enclose filling.

5 Repeat with remaining pastry and filling. Place triangles on baking tray and bake at 400°F for 15–20 minutes or until the pastry is golden brown.

PER 2 SAMOSAS: *Energy 338 kJ (81 Cal); Protein 2g (12%); Carbohydrates 12g (65%); Sugars 1g; Fat 2g (23%); Fibre 2g; Sodium 223mg; Calcium 13mg.*

MAKES 16 SAMOSAS

15oz can asparagus spears
1 clove garlic
1 tbsp ground almonds
dash of paprika

Asparagus Sauce

1 Place all ingredients in food processor or blender and process until smooth. If needed, add a little water. Pour into a saucepan and boil until mixture reaches desired consistency. Pour over steamed vegetables.

PER SERVE: *Energy 203 kJ (48 Cal); Protein 3g (22%); Carbohydrates 2g (30%); Sugars 1g; Fat 1g (48%); Fibre 3g; Sodium 204mg; Calcium 22mg.*

SERVES 4

Basic Stir-fry

1–2 tbsp sesame oil
3 cups mushrooms, thickly sliced
3 medium carrots, thinly sliced
6 tbsp water
1 medium broccoli head, thinly sliced
2 cups snow peas, trimmed and thickly sliced
4 tbsp low-salt soya sauce
4 spring onions, sliced thinly
1 tbsp sesame seeds (optional)

1 Heat oil in frying pan. Stir-fry mushrooms and carrots for 2 minutes. Add water and stir-fry for 5 minutes.

2 Add broccoli and snow peas.

3 Stir-fry until carrot and broccoli are just tender. Stir in soya sauce.

4 Serve with spring onion and sesame seeds.

PER SERVE: *Energy 718 kJ (172 Cal); Protein 12g (29%); Carbohydrates 8g (32%); Sugars 6g; Fat 8g (39%); Fibre 11g; Sodium 324mg; Calcium 84mg.*

SERVES 4

Spring Stir-fry

1 tsp oil
1 clove garlic, crushed
1 inch fresh ginger, peeled
and finely chopped
2–3 carrots,
cut into matchsticks
15oz can baby corn, drained
1 medium zucchini, cut into
large matchsticks
1 generous cup of green
beans, trimmed,
1 generous cup of snow peas,
trimmed
1 bunch asparagus, cut into
2–3-inch lengths
8 spring onions, trimmed and
cut into 2-inch lengths
½ basket cherry tomatoes

Sauce:
2 lemons, juiced
1 tbsp honey
1 tbsp low-salt soya sauce
1 tsp sesame oil

1 Heat oil in a large frying pan. Add garlic and ginger, and stir-fry for about 1 minute. Add carrots, baby corn, zucchini and beans, and stir-fry for 3–4 minutes. Add snow peas, asparagus, spring onion and cherry tomatoes, and stir-fry for 1–3 minutes.

2 Mix sauce ingredients in a small bowl, then add to stir-fry mixture. Stir well and cover the pan. Cook for 2–3 minutes more until the vegetable are just tender but still crisp.

PER SERVE: *Energy 558 kJ (133 Cal); Protein 7g (22%); Carbohydrates 15g (58%); Sugars 13g; Fat 3g (20%); Fibre 7g; Sodium 1373mg; Calcium 75mg.*

SERVES 4

Udon Noodle Stir-fry

1lb Udon noodles

1 tbsp oil

3 spring onions, cut into 2-inch lengths

2 onions, sliced

3 cloves garlic, crushed

1 tbsp fresh ginger, grated

2 carrots, sliced

5oz snow peas

1 tbsp water

4oz bean sprouts

1lb bok choy, cut into 2-inch lengths

2 tbsp low-salt soya sauce

1 Add noodles to a pot of boiling water and cook for about 5 minutes until tender. Drain and rinse under hot water.

2 Heat oil in pan or wok, then add onion, spring onions, garlic and ginger. Stir-fry over high heat for 1–2 minutes or until soft. Add carrot, snow peas and 1 tbsp of water. Toss well. Cover and cook for 1–2 minutes or until just tender.

3 Add noodles, bok choy, bean sprouts and soya sauce. Toss until bok choy is wilted and coated with sauce.

PER SERVE: *Energy 1889 kJ (451 Cal); Protein 18g (16%); Carbohydrates 77g (73%); Sugars 9g; Fat 5g (11%); Fibre 9g; Sodium 319mg; Calcium 136mg.*

SERVES 4

Vegetable Stir-fry

¼ cup almonds
1 large onion, chopped
1 tsp crushed garlic
1½ tsp freshly-grated ginger
1 tbsp water
2 cups sliced mushrooms
1 small bunch bok choy, sliced
1 red bell pepper, seeded and sliced
1 cup snow peas, trimmed
15oz can cooked chick peas (or other legume), drained and rinsed
¾ cup water
1 tsp all-purpose flour
1 tbsp low-salt soya sauce
1 cup mung bean sprouts

1 Dry roast almonds by placing on dry oven tray and baking at 350°F for 5–8 minutes or until the almonds are slightly brown.

2 Place onions, garlic, ginger and water in medium frying pan and stir-fry until onion is soft. Add mushrooms, bok choy, bell pepper, snow peas and chick peas. Stir-fry for 2–3 minutes.

3 Combine water, all-purpose flour and soya sauce, and stir through the vegetables. Cook until the mixture comes to the boil and sauce thickens a little. Add mung bean sprouts and fold through.

4 Serve on bed of rice or couscous and top with almonds.

PER SERVE: *Energy 631 kJ (151 Cal); Protein 9g (23%); Carbohydrates 14g (45%); Sugars 3g; Fat 5g (32%); Fibre 6g; Sodium 271mg; Calcium 69mg.*

SERVES 6

Sweet-n-Sour Tofu

10–13oz firm tofu, cubed
2 cloves garlic, crushed
2 tsp grated fresh ginger
2 tbsp low-salt soya sauce
¼ cup water
¼ cup flour
cooking spray
1 tsp oil
1 onion, cut in eighths
1 medium carrot, sliced
½ red bell pepper, sliced
1 zucchini, sliced
14oz can unsweetened pineapple pieces, drained and juice reserved
2 tbsp tomato paste
2 tbsp lemon juice
1 tbsp brown sugar (or honey)
1 tbsp all-purpose flour
½ cup water

1 Marinate tofu with the garlic, ginger, soya sauce and water in a covered container for at least 1 hour.

2 Drain tofu, saving the marinade. Dip the tofu in flour, spray a frying pan with oil and fry tofu on both sides until golden brown.

3 Saute onion, carrot, bell pepper and zucchini for 2–3 minutes. Add pineapple juice, tomato paste, lemon juice, sugar and marinade from tofu.

3 Bring to boil, reduce heat and add combined all-purpose flour and water. Stir until mixture boils and thickens. Add tofu and pineapple, then heat through.

4 Serve with brown rice.

PER SERVE: *Energy 844 kJ (202 Cal); Protein 11g (22%); Carbohydrates 22g (51%); Sugars 19g; Fat 6g (27%); Fibre 5g; Sodium 337mg; Calcium 141mg.*

SERVES 4

Tofu Vegetable Frittata

3 large bell peppers (different colors if possible), halved and deseeded
2 onions, cut in quarters
1 small broccoli head, broken into flowerets and lightly steamed

Sauce:
*1 cup water
*¾ cup raw cashews
2 tbsp flake yeast
1 tbsp dried onion flakes
10oz firm tofu
2 cloves garlic, crushed
1–2 tbsp all-purpose flour
¼ tsp tumeric (for color)
salt to taste

* May substitute 3–4 tbsp unsweetened soy milk for these ingredients.

1 Place bell pepper skin-side up under preheated hot grill. Cook for 8–10 minutes or until charred and blistered. Add onions for last 3–4 minutes. Transfer bell pepper to a sealed plastic bag and stand for 10 minutes. Preheat oven to 325°F. Peel the skin from the bell pepper and slice the flesh. Place all vegetables in a baking dish.

2 Blend sauce ingredients until smooth and consistency of thick yoghurt. Pour mixture over the vegetables and smooth over the top, making sure the middle is a little shallower than the sides so it cooks through.

3 Bake for 20–25 minutes, until the top is lightly golden. Turn off oven and leave in the oven for another 10–15 minutes to give it time to set and finish cooking without burning. Serve hot.

PER SERVE: *Energy 623 kJ (149 Cal); Protein 8g (21%); Carbohydrates 9g (29%); Sugars 4g; Fat 8g (50%); Fibre 3g; Sodium 15mg; Calcium 62mg.*

SERVES 8

Tofu Vegie Burgers

1 tbsp water
1 large onion, chopped
1 garlic clove, crushed
2 tsp tomato paste
4 tbsp whole wheat flour
½–1 tsp salt
3 tbsp walnuts, finely chopped
1 large carrot, grated
1 tsp curry paste or powder
2 tsp coriander
7oz firm tofu

1 Heat water in a large frying pan. Add carrot and onion, and cook for 3–4 minutes or until softened, stirring all the time. Add coriander, garlic, curry and tomato paste, and fry for a further 2 minutes, stirring all the time.

2 Mash the tofu or chop in a food processor and add to vegetables. Add flour, nuts and salt. Mix thoroughly until mixture starts to stick together. Remove from heat and let cool.

3 Shape the mixture into eight burgers or smaller portions.

4 Oil a baking tray and place burgers on tray. Bake at 350ºF for 20 minutes, turning after 10 minutes.

5 Serve in buns with hummus, lettuce and tomato, or with a salad.

Variation: Try other herbs in the place of curry powder and coriander.

PER SERVE: *Energy 317 kJ (75 Cal); Protein 4g (20%); Carbohydrates 5g (33%); Sugars 2g; Fat 4g (47%); Fibre 2g; Sodium 185mg; Calcium 44mg.*

SERVES 6–8

Vegetarian Quiche

5 sheets filo pastry
spray cooking oil
1 cup water
½lb soft tofu, rinsed and drained
1 tbsp lemon juice
1 tsp basil (optional)
¼ tsp turmeric
1 tbsp yeast flakes
2 tbsp all-purpose flour
½ cup raw cashew nuts
½–¾ tsp salt
1 clove garlic
12oz can asparagus spears, drained
1 onion, finely chopped
1 tsp oil

1 Blend all ingredients—except pastry, oil, asparagus and onion— until smooth.

2 Spray 9-inch quiche dish with cooking oil. Lay one sheet filo pastry in the dish, then spray with oil. Put another sheet on top and spray with oil. Repeat until all sheets of pastry are used. Gently press pastry into bottom of the dish and leave pastry overhanging the edges.

3 Saute onion until tender. Cover pastry base with onion and asparagus. Fill pastry dish with blended mixture. Trim or fold the pastry under.

4 Bake at 275°F for one hour, or until quiche is firm and golden.

PER SERVE: *Energy 450 kJ (108 Cal); Protein 5g (20%); Carbohydrates 8g (35%); Sugars 1.6g; Fat 5.5g (45%); Fibre 3g; Sodium 251mg; Calcium 38mg.*

SERVES 10

Vegetable Kebabs

small mushrooms
cherry tomatoes
zucchini
bell pepper
eggplant
red onion

sauce of your choice

1 Cut vegetables into pieces. Thread onto skewers and place on a double-sided grill like a Panini Maker. Cook until vegetables are just tender. Serve with a sauce of your choice.

Note: Use whatever vegetables are in your fridge at the time. Kebabs can be grilled, or baked in a hot oven or in a frying pan.

PER SERVE: *Energy 127 kJ (30 Cal); Protein 2g (31%); Carbohydrates 4g (58%); Sugars 3g; Fat 1g (11%); Fibre 3g; Sodium 9mg; Calcium 23mg.*

SERVES 6

Vegie Wrap Stack

5 tortilla wraps
13oz low-salt tomato pasta
sauce
4–5 cups of assorted,
thickly-sliced, cooked
vegetables, such as kumara
(sweet potato), potato,
zucchini, chargrilled
eggplant, bell pepper and
fresh spinach
fresh basil leaves (optional)

1 Lay a wrap in the bottom of a baking dish. Spread with pasta sauce and place a layer of vegetables on the wrap. Repeat layers until all the wraps and vegetables are used.

2 Pour the remainder of the pasta sauce over the vegetables on top of the final wrap.

3 Cover with tinfoil and bake at 350°F for 20–30 minutes. Remove from the oven and leave to stand for a few minutes. Serve garnished with fresh basil leaves.

PER SERVE: *Energy 617 kJ (147 Cal); Protein 5g (13%); Carbohydrates 27g (81%); Sugars 6g; Fat 1g (6%); Fibre 5g; Sodium 245mg; Calcium 72mg.*

SERVES 6

Dips and sauces

Basil Pesto Sauce

1 cup cashews
¾ cup water
1 tsp salt
1–2 lemons, juiced
1 tsp paprika
1–3 cloves garlic
2 cups roughly-chopped
fresh basil

1 Place ingredients in blender or food processor and blend until smooth.

PER SERVE: *Energy 385 kJ (92 Cal); Protein 3g (13%); Carbohydrates 3g (17%); Sugars 1g; Fat 7g (70%); Fibre 1g; Sodium 232mg; Calcium 25mg.*

SERVES 10

Eggplant Dip

1 eggplant
1–2 lemons, juiced
1 tbsp tahini
1 clove garlic (optional)
1 tsp olive oil (optional)
salt to taste (optional)

1 Pierce eggplant with a knife several times, then microwave on high until tender (about 4 minutes).
2 Scoop out eggplant flesh and blend in food processor with lemon juice, tahini, garlic and oil until smooth.

3 Season with salt to taste and add more lemon juice, if necessary.

PER SERVE: *Energy 86 kJ (16 Cal); Protein 1g (16%); Carbohydrates 1g (31%); Sugars 1g; Fat 1g (53%); Fibre 1g; Sodium 3mg; Calcium 15mg.*

SERVES 10

Guacamole

2 avocados, deseeded and peeled
2 tbsp lemon juice (to taste)
1 spring onion, chopped
salt to taste

1 Place avocados and spring onions in a food processor.
2 Add lemon juice and process until smooth.
3 Season to taste.

PER SERVE: *Energy 435 kJ (104 Cal); Protein 1g (4%); Carbohydrates 0.5g (3%); Sugars 0.5g; Fat 11g (93%); Fibre 1g; Sodium 59mg; Calcium 12mg.*

SERVES 10

Hummus with Sundried Tomatoes

15oz can chickpeas, drained
1 tbsp tahini
2 cloves garlic
2 tbsp finely-chopped
sundried tomatoes
1 tbsp olive oil
1 tbsp tomato paste
½ tsp cumin
¼ tsp ground coriander
juice of 1–2 lemons

1 Place all ingredients except lemon juice in a food processor or blender and blend for approximately 1 minute.

2 Add lemon juice and blend until smooth. Refrigerate up to 3 days.

PER SERVE: *Energy 358 kJ (62 Cal); Protein 3g (17%); Carbohydrates 5g (40%); Sugars 1g; Fat 3g (43%); Fibre 2g; Sodium 88mg; Calcium 27mg.*

SERVES 10

Kumara Hummus

½ cup cooked kumara (sweet
potato) or pumpkin
1 clove garlic
15oz can chickpeas
¼–½ tsp curry powder or
cumin
3 tbsp peanut butter
3 tbsp lemon juice
¼–½ tsp salt (optional)
¼ cup liquid from chickpeas

1 Place garlic and chickpeas in a blender or food processor, and process until finely chopped.

2 Add kumara, curry powder or cumin, peanut butter and lemon juice.

3 Process until evenly mixed, then add two tablespoons of the chickpea liquid and salt.

4 Process until very smooth, adding extra chickpea liquid if necessary.

5 Taste and add extra salt, if needed.

PER SERVE: *Energy 373 kJ (89 Cal); Protein 4g (20%); Carbohydrates 8g (43%); Sugars 1g; Fat 4g (37%); Fibre 3g; Sodium 124mg; Calcium 26mg.*

SERVES 10

Red Kidney Bean Dip

15oz can red kidney beans,
rinsed and drained
(save liquid)
2 cloves garlic, crushed
1 tbsp tomato paste
½ tsp paprika
½ cup sundried tomatoes,
finely chopped
lemon juice (optional)
salt (optional)

1 Place beans, garlic, tomato paste, paprika and sundried tomatoes in food processor. Blend until well chopped.

2 Add saved bean liquid and mix to desired consistency.

3 Season with salt and lemon juice to taste.

PER SERVE: *Energy 212 kJ (51 Cal); Protein 3g (25%); Carbohydrates 7g (68%); Sugars 2g; Fat 0.4g (7%); Fibre 3g; Sodium 140mg; Calcium 18mg.*

SERVES 10

Roasted Red Capsicum Hummus

15oz can chickpeas, drained (save liquid)
1 roasted red bell pepper or ½ cup ready-roasted bell pepper (capsicum)
2 cloves garlic
1 tbsp tahini
juice of 1–2 lemons
2 spring onions
2 tbsp parsley
½ tsp ground cumin
½ tsp coriander

1 Puree ingredients in a food processor, thinning with some of the liquid from the chickpeas if it is too thick.

2 Refrigerate 3 to 4 days.

PER SERVE: *Energy 290 kJ (69 Cal); Protein 4g (21%); Carbohydrates 7g (49%); Sugars 2g; Fat 2g (30%); Fibre 3g; Sodium 112mg; Calcium 34mg.*

SERVES 10

Fresh salads

Almond Coleslaw

3 cups finely-shredded
green cabbage
½ cup diced cucumber
½ cup sliced celery
6 spring onions, chopped
finely
¼ cup low-fat salad dressing
(of your choice)
1 tbsp tomato juice
1 tbsp lemon juice
¼ cup slivered almonds

1 Combine vegetables.

2 Mix salad dressing, tomato juice and lemon juice.

3 Just before serving, fold the dressing and nuts through the vegetables.

PER SERVE: *Energy 286 kJ (68 Cal); Protein 2g (12%); Carbohydrates 5g (39%); Sugars 5g; Fat 4g (49%); Fibre 3g; Sodium 130mg; Calcium 39mg.*

SERVES 6

Bean and Pasta Salad

1½ cups uncooked pasta

10oz can mixed beans, drained and rinsed

1 cup green beans

2 tomatoes, chopped

2 spring onions, chopped

12 black olives, sliced

Dressing:

¼ cup lemon juice

1 tbsp olive oil

1 clove garlic, crushed

1 tbsp finely chopped fresh basil leaves

1 Cook pasta according to instructions on the packet. Steam green beans until tender, then drain. Rinse beans and pasta under cold water and drain.

2 In a large bowl, mix pasta, mixed beans, green beans, tomatoes, spring onions and olives.

3 Place all dressing ingredients in a screw-top jar and shake well.

4 Add dressing to salad. Toss gently and serve.

PER SERVE: *Energy 1080 kJ (258 Cal); Protein 7g (12%); Carbohydrates 35g (59%); Sugars 6g; Fat 8g (29%); Fibre 5g; Sodium 383mg; Calcium 41mg.*

SERVES 6

Beet Salad

2 carrots, grated
1 large beet, peeled and grated
2 tbsp pumpkin seeds
2 tbsp sunflower seeds
¼ cup light vinaigrette
salt and pepper to taste (optional)
leaf lettuce to serve

1 Combine carrot, beet, pumpkin seeds, sunflower seeds and vinaigrette in a bowl.

2 Season to taste. Serve on a bed of leaf lettuce.

PER SERVE: *Energy 681 kJ (163 Cal); Protein 3g (9%); Carbohydrates 8g (23%); Sugars 7g; Fat 12g (68%); Fibre 3g; Sodium 172mg; Calcium 33mg.*

SERVES 4

Couscous and Chickpea Salad

1 cup couscous
¼ cup currants
1¼ cups boiling water
15oz can chickpeas, rinsed
and drained
1 red bell pepper, chopped
2 spring onions, sliced
½ cup olives
2–3 tbsp chopped mint

Dressing:
5 fl oz orange juice
2 tbsp apple cider or balsamic
vinegar
1–2 tsp ground cumin
½ tsp salt
1 clove garlic, crushed
parsley (optional)

1 Place couscous and currants in a bowl, and cover with boiling water. Cover the bowl and leave for 5 minutes.

2 Mix chickpeas, bell pepper, spring onions, olives and mint through the couscous.

3 Combine dressing ingredients and mix well. Pour dressing over salad and mix well. Garnish with mint, parsley or oregano.

PER SERVE: *Energy 926 kJ (221 Cal); Protein 8g (14%); Carbohydrates 36g (71%); Sugars 8g; Fat 4g (15%); Fibre 5g; Sodium 815mg; Calcium 62mg.*

SERVES 6

Greek Salad

5 tomatoes
1 cucumber
½ red onion
½ cup black olives
3oz baby spinach
juice of 1 lemon

1 Cut tomatoes into wedges. Cut cucumber in half, then in ⅛-inch diagonal slices. Thinly slice the red onion. Combine the tomatoes, cucumber, red onion, black olives and spinach in a serving bowl.

2 Squeeze lemon juice over the salad. Toss and serve.

PER SERVE: *Energy 201 kJ (48 Cal); Protein 2g (19%); Carbohydrates 7g (74%); Sugars 7g; Fat 0.4g (7%); Fibre 3g; Sodium 127mg; Calcium 31mg.*

SERVES 6

Green Vegetable Salad

2 cups green beans, trimmed
2 cups snow peas, trimmed
2–3 cups mixed salad greens
¼ cup loosely-packed flat leaf parsley leaves (optional)

Dressing:
1 tbsp yellow mustard
2–4 tbsp lemon juice
1 tsp sugar
1 tbsp oil

1 Steam or microwave beans and peas separately with a little water.

2 When tender, drain and rinse under cold water. Toss together beans, peas, salad greens and parsley in a large bowl.

3 Place dressing ingredients in a small bowl and mix well. Drizzle salad with dressing just before serving.

PER SERVE: *Energy 290 kJ (69 Cal); Protein 2g (13%); Carbohydrates 5g (40%); Sugars 4g; Fat 4g (47%); Fibre 3g; Sodium 66mg; Calcium 55mg.*

SERVES 4

Kumara Salad

2 kumara (sweet potato), cut into cubes
1½ tbsp olive oil
1 tbsp orange juice
2 spring onions, thinly sliced
2 small oranges, peeled and cubed
1 tsp garlic powder
(or 1 clove of garlic, crushed)

1 Steam, boil or microwave kumara until just soft but not mushy.

2 When cooled, place in another bowl, add remaining ingredients and mix until just combined.

3 Leave to sit in refrigerator for 30 minutes before serving.

PER SERVE: *Energy 606 kJ (145 Cal); Protein 2g (5%); Carbohydrates 21g (63%); Sugars 7g; Fat 5g (32%); Fibre 3g; Sodium 21mg; Calcium 25mg.*

SERVES 4

Mixed Bean Salad

15oz can mixed beans, rinsed
and drained
1 red bell pepper, diced
1 red onion, sliced thinly
½ cup black olives
1 lemon, juiced
1 cup diced celery
3 cups corn kernels, cooked
1 cup green beans, cooked

1 Mix ingredients in large bowl. Refrigerate until ready to serve.

PER SERVE: *Energy 806 kJ (192 Cal); Protein 8g (17%); Carbohydrates 32g (77%); Sugars 9g; Fat 1g (6%); Fibre 8g; Sodium 320mg; Calcium 51mg.*

SERVES 6

Open Sandwich

1 slice of wholegrain bread
red bell pepper hummus
1 small tomato
4 slices cucumber
¼ cup mixed lettuce and bean
sprouts

1 Spread hummus evenly over bread and put all other ingredients on top.
Variation: Try different fillings to create entirely different meals.

PER SERVE: *Energy 650 kJ (155 Cal); Protein 7g (18%); Carbohydrates 19g (57%); Sugars 6g; Fat 4g (25%); Fibre 6g; Sodium 211mg; Calcium 46mg.*

SERVES 1

Pear Pecan Salad

3 cups spinach, torn
1 medium pear, sliced
1 cup red seedless grapes
½ cup celery, sliced
½ cup pecan pieces

Dressing:
½ cup lemon juice
1 tbsp olive oil
2 tbsp honey

1 In a large bowl, mix all salad ingredients.

2 In another bowl, mix dressing ingredients and refrigerate.

3 Just before serving, drizzle dressing over salad and toss.

Variation: To lower the fat content of this salad, omit pecans.

PER SERVE: *Energy 976 kJ (233 Cal); Protein 3g (5%); Carbohydrates 21g (39%); Sugars 20g; Fat 15g (56%); Fibre 4g; Sodium 71mg; Calcium 61mg.*

SERVES 4

Quinoa Salad

1 cup uncooked quinoa
2 tsp ground cumin
2 cups water
15oz can kidney beans, drained
1½ cup corn kernels, cooked
1 red bell pepper, diced
½ cup sliced red onion
¼ cup chopped parsley
olives to taste, chopped
1 tbsp oil
2–3 tbsp lemon juice
salt and pepper to taste

1 Rinse quinoa in strainer, then drain.

2 In medium saucepan, combine cumin and water. Add the quinoa and bring to the boil.

3 Reduce to simmer, cover and cook until all the water is absorbed (15–20 minutes).

4 Fluff with a fork and place quinoa in a bowl. Add beans, corn, bell pepper, parsley, onion and olives, and mix well. Stir in oil and lemon juice. Season to taste. Serve at room temperature.

PER SERVE: *Energy 1113 kJ (265 Cal); Protein 11g (16%); Carbohydrates 41g (72%); Sugars 7g; Fat 4g (12%); Fibre 10g; Sodium 318mg; Calcium 61mg.*

SERVES 6

Red Cabbage and Orange Salad

4 cups shredded red cabbage
3 oranges, peeled and sliced
4 spring onions, sliced
1 avocado, peeled and sliced
2 cups broccoli florets
¼ cup walnuts, chopped
(optional)

Dressing:
juice of 1 orange
1 tsp crushed garlic
1 tsp gourmet mustard
1 tbsp olive oil
1 tbsp balsamic vinegar

1 Steam broccoli until just cooked, then strain and put aside to cool. Place oranges and avocado in a serving bowl with shredded cabbage and spring onions. Add cooled broccoli and walnuts to the salad and mix.

2 In another bowl, mix dressing ingredients and drizzle over salad.

Variation: To reduce the fat content of this salad, omit nuts and avocado.

PER SERVE: *Energy 723 kJ (172 Cal); Protein 5g (11%); Carbohydrates 10g (29%); Sugars 9g; Fat 12g (60%); Fibre 6g; Sodium 28mg; Calcium 61mg.*

SERVES 6

Summer Salad

1 avocado, cubed
2–3 tomatoes, cut into wedges
half a cucumber, cubed
1 small packet mixed lettuce
or baby spinach
1–2 spring onions, thinly sliced

Dressing:
2–3 tbsp lemon juice
½ tsp sugar (optional)
¼ tsp salt (optional)

1 Place salad ingredients in a large salad bowl.

2 Mix dressing ingredients in a screw-top jar and shake together. Pour over salad and gently toss until all coated with the dressing.

Variation: To reduce the fat content of this recipe, omit avocado.

PER SERVE: *Energy 664 kJ (159 Cal); Protein 3g (9%); Carbohydrates 4g (13%); Sugars 4g; Fat 14g (78%); Fibre 3g; Sodium 20mg; Calcium 60mg.*

SERVES 4

Tabbouleh

1 cup bulgur wheat
2 cups boiling water
1 red bell pepper, chopped
1 cup cherry tomatoes, cut in half
¼ cup fresh basil or parsley, chopped
2 cups cucumber, finely chopped
½ tsp salt
1 lemon, juiced and a little bit of zest
1 tbsp olive oil
15oz can chickpeas, drained

1 Pour boiling water over bulgur wheat and let stand while preparing the other vegetables (for at least 30 minutes). Drain carefully, add remaining ingredients and mix.

Serving suggestion: Serve on a lettuce leaf or use to fill pita bread.

PER SERVE: *Energy 689 kJ (164 Cal); Protein 6g (15%); Carbohydrates 23g (64%); Sugars 3g; Fat 4g (21%); Fibre 7g; Sodium 340mg; Calcium 48mg.*

SERVES 4–6

Tossed Beet Greens Salad

1 handful beet greens (or
fresh beet leaves)
1 red bell pepper, finely
sliced
2–3 spring onions, finely sliced
2 tbsp mint
1 handful bean sprouts
¼ cup slivered almonds
(optional)

Dressing:
1 tbsp lemon juice
2 tsp olive oil
1 tbsp balsamic vinegar
½ tsp sugar
1 clove garlic, crushed
salt and pepper to taste

1 Toast slivered almonds until lightly brown, then allow to cool. Finely slice beet greens, bell pepper, spring onions and mint. Place in a salad bowl with bean sprouts and almonds.

2 Mix dressing ingredients and drizzle over salad.

PER SERVE: *Energy 372 kJ (89 Cal); Protein 3g (15%); Carbohydrates 4g (23%); Sugars 3g; Fat 6g (62%); Fibre 3g; Sodium 34mg; Calcium 43mg.*

SERVES 4

Tossed Vegetable Salad

1 bunch asparagus
2 cups baby green beans
2 small red bell peppers
2 baby eggplants, halved

Dressing:
1 tbsp oil
3 tbsp lemon juice
1/3 cup parsley, chopped
1 clove garlic, crushed
2 tbsp pine nuts (optional)
1 cup baby spinach (optional)

1 Cut asparagus spears in half and cut thick pieces in half lengthways. Blanch asparagus and beans in boiling water for about 1 minute or until just tender. Drain and rinse under cold water.

2 Cut bell peppers into quarters, then remove and discard seeds. Grill bell pepper and eggplant until browned and tender. Cool to room temperature, and slice bell pepper and eggplant thickly.

3 Place vegetables into a bowl. Add combined oil, juice, parsley and garlic. Toss to combine with spinach. Serve warm, sprinkled with pine nuts.

PER SERVE: *Energy 318 kJ (76 Cal); Protein 4g (20%); Carbohydrates 5g (36%); Sugars 4g; Fat 4g (44%); Fibre 4g; Sodium 7mg; Calcium 54mg.*

SERVES 4

Watercress Potato Salad

15oz new baby potatoes, unpeeled
1 bunch watercress
1 basket cherry tomatoes, halved
2 tbsp pumpkin seeds

Dressing:
5oz soft or silken tofu
1 tbsp oil
4 tbsp lemon juice
1½ tsp honey or sugar
¾ tsp onion powder

1 Boil potatoes until just tender, then drain and leave to cool. In a large bowl, gently toss together potatoes, watercress, tomatoes and pumpkin seeds.

2 Place dressing ingredients into a blender or food processor and blend until creamy. Store in refrigerator until ready to serve. Just before serving, drizzle dressing over salad.

PER SERVE: *Energy 827 kJ (198 Cal); Protein 9g (18%); Carbohydrates 20g (45%); Sugars 5g; Fat 8g (37%); Fibre 5g; Sodium 20mg; Calcium 158mg.*

SERVES 4

Desserts

Apple Cake

3 medium apples, peeled and
sliced thinly
2 tbsp water
½ cup sugar
½ cup margarine
½ cup unsweetened apple
sauce
2 tbsp non-dairy milk
1 cup all-purpose flour
½ cup whole wheat flour
2½ tsp baking powder

Topping:
¼ cup brown sugar
½ tsp cinnamon
½ tsp ground ginger

1 Preheat oven to 350°F and grease a 9-inch spring-form cake tin.

2 Cook apples in water on stove or in microwave until they are just a little soft but not mushy (microwave 1½ minutes on high), then set aside.

3 Cream margarine and sugar, add apple sauce and milk, then mix again. Add flour and baking powder. Stir until just combined.

4 Pour batter into the prepared pan and arrange apple slices on top.

5 Mix together brown sugar, cinnamon and ginger. Sprinkle mixture over the top of apple slices.

6 Bake for 30–40 minutes or until a toothpick comes out clean. Allow cake to cool for 15 minutes before removing from tin. This cake is best eaten on the day it is made.

Variation: Replace ½ cup of margarine with an extra ½ cup of unsweetened apple sauce.

PER SERVE: *Energy 1059 kJ (253 Cal); Protein 3g (4%); Carbohydrates 37g (61%); Sugars 22g; Fat 10g (35%); Fibre 2g; Sodium 239mg; Calcium 26mg.*

SERVES 8–10

Apricot and Passionfruit Custard Tartlets

Filo cups:
3 sheets filo pastry
1 tbsp oil or oil spray

Filling:
1 cup custard (1 cup non-dairy milk, ½ tbsp custard powder, 2 tsp sugar)
grated rind of one orange
15oz can apricots in juice
passionfruit pulp

1 Preheat oven to 400°F.

2 Brush half of one sheet of filo with oil and fold sheet in half. Repeat with other sheets. Cut each sheet into four squares. Line greased jumbo muffin tins using two squares of pastry for each tartlet.

3 Bake for 5 minutes until lightly golden. Allow to cool. These will keep in an airtight container for several days.

4 Combine custard and orange rind. Fill filo cups with custard. Arrange apricot halves on top and drizzle with passionfruit pulp.

PER SERVE: *Energy 402 kJ (96 Cal); Protein 3g (11%); Carbohydrates 13g (58%); Sugars 9g; Fat 3g (31%); Fibre 2g; Sodium 86mg; Calcium 22mg.*

SERVES 6

Apricot Dessert Cake

2 x 15oz cans apricots in juice
¼ cup rice bran oil
1 heaped tsp no-egg replacer powder
½ cup soy milk
¾ cup juice from apricots
¼ teaspoon almond essence
⅓ cup white sugar
1 cup self-raising flour
½ cup whole wheat flour
¼ cup almonds, chopped

Fruit custard:
2 cups orange juice
2 tbsp custard powder, dissolved in extra fruit juice from apricots

1 Preheat oven to 375°F. Drain apricots, reserving the juice.

2 Mix oil, no-egg replacement powder, soy milk, almond essence and ¾ cup reserved juice.

3 Keep a few of the apricots for later but chop the rest finely and add to the liquid mixture, along with the sugar and flour. Fold together, being careful not to over mix.

4 Pour the mixture into prepared baking dish, and place reserved apricots on top in a nice pattern. Sprinkle with chopped almonds and bake for 25–30 minutes until center is cooked and golden.

Fruit custard:

1 Heat orange juice in medium saucepan. Mix in custard powder mixture and stir until thickened.

2 Serve cake warm, with custard.

PER SERVE: *Energy 1399 kJ (334 Cal); Protein 5g (6%); Carbohydrates 44g (56%); Sugars 25g; Fat 14g (38%); Fibre 4g; Sodium 310mg; Calcium 46mg.*

SERVES 6–8

Berri-fu Pie

Crust:
¾ cup pitted dates
¼ cup water
¾ cup cornflakes, crushed
½ cup quick oats
3 tbsp almonds, finely chopped

Filling:
2 cups silken tofu
1 tbsp lemon juice
1 tbsp vanilla
15oz can unsweetened
crushed pineapple
3 tbsp all-purpose flour
1 medium banana
½ cup honey

Topping:
2 cups frozen blueberries or
strawberries
⅓ cup water
2 tbsp all-purpose flour

1 Bring dates and water to the boil. Reduce to low heat and simmer, covered, for 5 minutes until soft. Add remaining crust ingredients to date mixture and mix well. Press mixture into the bottom of a lightly oiled 9-inch spring-form tin. Set aside.

2 Place tofu, lemon juice, vanilla and half the pineapple in a blender. Blend until smooth, then pour into a bowl. Place the remaining pineapple, all-purpose flour, banana and honey into blender and process until smooth. Pour into bowl with other half of the fillings and mix together well.

3 Pour filling into crust. Bake at 350°F for 45 minutes until edges are browned and the center is firm. Cool to room temperature.

4 In a small saucepan, mix frozen berries, water and all-purpose flour. Cook over medium heat until it has thickened and is clear. Spread the fruit mixture over the top of the cooled pie. Chill before serving.

PER SERVE: *Energy 1062 kJ (254 Cal); Protein 7g (11%); Carbohydrates 43g (73%); Sugars 34g; Fat 5g (16%); Fibre 5g; Sodium 18mg; Calcium 84mg.*

SERVES 10

Berry Banana Crumble

3 bananas
10oz frozen raspberries
2 tbsp honey
3 tbsp low-fat margarine
½ cup whole wheat flour
½ cup rolled oats
3 tbsp brown sugar
¼ cup flaked almonds

1 Preheat oven to 350°F.

2 Slice bananas and place with raspberries in ovenproof dish. Drizzle with honey.

3 In a separate bowl, mix flour and sugar. Rub margarine into flour mixture and add rolled oats.

4 Sprinkle crumble mixture over bananas and berries. Sprinkle flaked almonds over crumble mixture. Bake for 25–30 minutes or until golden brown.

5 Serve with soy yoghurt, dairy-free ice-cream or sorbet.

Variation: Use cooked apples, tinned peaches, apricots or any other fruit in place of the bananas and raspberries.

PER SERVE: *Energy 1006 kJ (240 Cal); Protein 5g (8%); Carbohydrates 37g (67%); Sugars 23g; Fat 7g (25%); Fibre 5g; Sodium 49mg; Calcium 36mg.*

SERVES 6

Nola's Chocolate Truffles

1 cup dates, chopped
juice of 1 orange
1 cup raisins or sultanas
¼ cup apricots, chopped
1 cup walnuts, finely chopped
2 tbsp cocoa or carob powder
1 tsp vanilla (optional)
1 tsp orange rind
½ tsp cinnamon (optional)
½ cup dark chocolate chips or carob chips
¼ cup desiccated coconut (for coating)

1 Place dates and orange juice in a bowl and microwave for 1 minute. Place with other ingredients in a food processor and process until the mixture clumps together.

2 Take level tablespoons of mixture, dip in coconut and roll into balls.

3 Refrigerate until firm. Store in the fridge for up to 2 weeks.

Variation: Use different dried fruits for different flavors. For special occasions, dip these truffles in dark chocolate or carob and leave to harden before eating

PER TRUFFLE: *Energy 450 kJ (108 Cal); Protein 2g (6%); Carbohydrates 13g (54%); Sugars 12g; Fat 5g (40%); Fibre 2g; Sodium 11mg; Calcium 16mg.*

MAKES 24 TRUFFLES

Chocolate Nut Cookies

1 cup rolled oats
1 cup whole wheat flour
½ tsp baking soda
½ tsp salt
½ cup dark chocolate chips or carob chips
½ cup sultanas
½ cup chopped nuts
½ cup canola oil
1 tbsp ground linseed
3 tbsp water
½ cup brown sugar
½ tsp vanilla

1 Preheat oven to 325°F.

2 Measure first 7 ingredients into a large bowl and stir to combine.

3 Place oil, linseed, water, vanilla and sugar in food processor, and whiz until pale and creamy. Pour onto dry ingredients and stir until thoroughly combined.

4 Form into walnut-sized balls and press onto an oil-sprayed tray.

5 Bake for 10–12 minutes until golden.

PER COOKIE: *Energy 529 kJ (126 Cal); Protein 2g (7%); Carbohydrates 13g (43%); Sugars 7g; Fat 7g (50%); Fibre 1g; Sodium 86mg; Calcium 16mg.*

MAKES 24 COOKIES

Orange Sauce

1 cup orange juice
1 passionfruit
1-2 tbsp all-purpose flour

1 Mix ingredients in a saucepan, and cook over a low heat until thickened and clear.

Note: Serve with Date and Orange Slice.

PER SERVE: *Energy 65 kJ (15 Cal); Protein 0.2g (5%); Carbohydrates 3.3g (93%); Sugars 2g; Fat 0g (2%); Fibre 0.3g; Sodium 2.3mg; Calcium 2.8mg.*

SERVES 10

Date and Orange Slice

Base:
½ cup rice bran oil
½ cup honey
1½ cups whole wheat flour
½ cup soy flour
½ tsp salt
1½ cups rolled oats
1 tsp cinnamon
1 tsp nutmeg
1 tsp baking powder

Filling:
2 cups dates, chopped
15oz can crushed pineapple in juice
½ cup chopped dried apricots
3 oranges (juice and rind)

Filling:
1 Mix all ingredients together in a saucepan and simmer over low heat until thickened. Cool.

Base:
1 Mix oil and honey. Add remaining ingredients and stir until mixed thoroughly. Place half of the mixture into a greased 12 x 8-inch dish, press to cover base of dish.

2 Spread cooled filling over base and cover with remaining crumb mixture.

3 Bake at 350°F for 30 minutes, until light brown.

4 Cool slightly and cut into bars.

Variation: Serve as a dessert with orange sauce or pineapple cream.

PER SERVE: *Energy 801 kJ (192 Cal); Protein 3g (7%); Carbohydrates 30g (67%); Sugars 21g; Fat 6g (26%); Fibre 4g; Sodium 70mg; Calcium 30mg.*

SERVES 24

Fruit Cake

2lb mixed dried fruit
2 cups orange juice
1 tsp almond essence
2–2½ cups self-raising flour

1 Soak fruit in orange juice overnight in covered container.

2 Preheat oven to 275°F.

3 Add 2 cups flour and almond essence to the fruit mixture and combine. Add extra flour if necessary to make a firm cake mixture. Place in a lined 8-inch cake tin and cook for 1½ hours. Cover the top with baking paper and cook for a further 1–1 ½ hours, until firm.

4 Best left for a day to let flavors develop before eating.

Note: This is a rich cake so serve in small slices.

PER SERVE: *Energy 616 kJ (147 Cal); Protein 2g (7%); Carbohydrates 32g (89%); Sugars 23g; Fat 0.4g (4%); Fibre 4g; Sodium 19mg; Calcium 31mg.*

SERVES 30

Fruit Rice

¾ cup sultanas
15oz can fruit in natural juice
1 cup brown rice
3 cups water

1 Preheat oven to 350°F.

2 Combine all ingredients in a casserole dish. Cover and bake for 2 hours. Serve cold or warm.

PER SERVE: *Energy 1368 kJ (327 Cal); Protein 5g (7%); Carbohydrates 70g (89%); Sugars 31g; Fat 1g (4%); Fibre 4g; Sodium 19mg; Calcium 31mg.*

SERVES 4

Pineapple Cream

½ cup pineapple juice
1 cup fresh or canned pineapple
½ cup raw cashews
1 tsp vanilla extract
pinch of salt

1 Place ingredients in a food processor. Process until thick and creamy, adding extra water if necessary.

Variation: Use pears in place of the pineapple for a completely different flavor.

PER SERVE: *Energy 232 kJ (55 Cal); Protein 1g (9%); Carbohydrates 4g (35%); Sugars 4g; Fat 3g (56%); Fibre 1g; Sodium 30mg; Calcium 5mg.*

SERVES 10

Fruit Salad

2 kiwi fruit, peeled and chopped
½ fresh pineapple, peeled and chopped
1–2 cups red grapes
2 oranges, peeled and cubed
1 basket strawberries
½ cantaloupe melon, peeled and cubed
passionfruit pulp (optional)

1 Mix all the fruit in a bowl and serve topped with passionfruit pulp, ice-cream or any dessert.

Variation: Use whatever fruit is seasonally available. If fruit is out of season, use canned fruit.

PER SERVE: *Energy 373 kJ (89 Cal); Protein 2g (7%); Carbohydrates 18g (89%); Sugars 18g; Fat 0.4g (4%); Fibre 4g; Sodium 8mg; Calcium 36mg.*

SERVES 4

Fruit Truffles

1 cup dried fruit of your choice
1 cup jumbo raisins
¾ cup cashew nut pieces
1 tsp lemon juice
1 tsp lemon rind
¼ tsp salt
¼ cup desiccated coconut
(for coating)

1 Place ingredients—except coconut—in a food processor and process for 1–2 minutes until the ingredients start to stick together. Process for another 15 seconds, adding a little water if mixture is too dry.

2 Place coconut in a bowl. Take teaspoon-sized portions of fruit mixture, shape into balls and roll in coconut. Place in airtight container and chill in fridge until ready to serve.

Note: These truffles are fairly rich, so make them small.

PER SERVE: *Energy 359 kJ (86 Cal); Protein 1g (6%); Carbohydrates 11g (58%); Sugars 10g; Fat 3g (36%); Fibre 2g; Sodium 37mg; Calcium 12mg.*

SERVES 20

Jaffa Nut Brownie

½ cup dates
1 orange (juice and rind)
1½ cups stewed apple, pureed
½ cup self-raising flour
½ cup whole wheat flour
½ tsp baking soda
⅓ cup cocoa or carob powder
¼ cup brown sugar
½ tsp salt
¾ cup nuts (almond, walnut or hazelnuts)
½ cup chocolate chips or carob chips

1 Preheat oven to 350°F. Place dates, orange rind and juice in a bowl, and microwave for 1 minute or until dates are soft. Allow to cool.

2 Place pureed apple and date mixture in a mixing bowl. Add all remaining ingredients and fold through until just mixed. Do not overmix. Grease an 7 x 11-inch baking dish. Transfer mixture and spread evenly. Bake 25–30 minutes until cooked but not overcooked.

3 Allow to cool completely before slicing.

Variation: Serve as a dessert with raspberry sauce and low-fat ice-cream.

PER SLICE: *Energy 539 kJ (129 Cal); Protein 2g (9%); Carbohydrates 17g (57%); Sugars 11g; Fat 5g (34%); Fibre 2g; Sodium 124mg; Calcium 24mg.*

MAKES 18 SLICES

Lemon Flan

Base:
5 slices wholegrain bread
½ cup desiccated coconut
½ cup dates

Filling:
½lb soft tofu, rinsed and drained
15oz can unsweetened pineapple pieces, including juice
¼ cup water
½ cup lemon juice
2 tsp lemon rind
½ cup honey
½ cup all-purpose flour
2 tbsp dessicated coconut

Base:

1 Place dates in small saucepan, just cover with water and boil for 5 minutes.

2 Place bread, coconut and softened dates in food processor. Process until chopped and mixed. Add a little liquid from the dates if the mixture is too dry to hold its shape.

3 Grease 8-inch square flan tin. Press base mixture into tin.

4 Bake at 350°F for 10–20 minutes until light golden color.

Filling:

1 Blend or process all ingredients until smooth. Pour into medium saucepan and boil until thickened.

Stir frequently so the mixture doesn't stick to the bottom of the pan.

2 Pour into baked base and smooth. Sprinkle with coconut.

3 Refrigerate several hours until set.

PER SERVE: *Energy 860 kJ (205 Cal); Protein 4g (8%); Carbohydrates 35g (71%); Sugars 22g; Fat 5g (21%); Fibre 3g; Sodium 99mg; Calcium 44mg.*

SERVES 12

Berry Smoothie

1 cup frozen berries
1 cup apple juice
1 tsp vanilla extract

1 Place berries in a food processor or blender and blend. Gradually add apple juice until smooth. Add vanilla, mix again and serve.

PER SERVE: *Energy 426 kJ (102 Cal); Protein 1g (2%); Carbohydrates 23g (95%); Sugars 23g; Fat 0g (3%); Fibre 2g; Sodium 17mg; Calcium 14mg.*

SERVES 2

Chocolate Banana Shake

1 cup non-dairy milk
2 ripe bananas, cut into
chunks and previously frozen
2 tbsp cocoa or carob powder
½ tsp vanilla extract
1 tsp sugar (optional)

1 Combine milk, frozen banana, cocoa and vanilla extract in a blender or food processer. Blend until everything is smooth and there are no lumps of cocoa. Add sugar to taste, if desired.

2 Pour shake into 2 tall glasses and garnish.

PER SERVE: *Energy 921 kJ (220 Cal); Protein 8g (14%); Carbohydrates 32g (63%); Sugars 22g; Fat 6g (23%); Fibre 4g; Sodium 103mg; Calcium 163mg.*

SERVES 2

Pear, Berry and Ginger Smoothie

1½ cups non-dairy milk
4 pear halves
1 cup frozen berries
1 tbsp honey
2 tbsp ground almonds
½ inch ginger root, peeled and sliced
½ tsp vanilla extract
5oz berry soy yoghurt (optional)

1 Place all ingredients in a blender and blend until smooth.

PER SERVE: *Energy 1317 kJ (315 Cal); Protein 9g (12%); Carbohydrates 40g (57%); Sugars 33g; Fat 11g (31%); Fibre 9g; Sodium 85mg; Calcium 269mg.*

SERVES 2

Breakfast

Apple and Spice Porridge

½ cup rolled oats
1½ cup water
1 apple, grated
4 dates or dried apricots, chopped
pinch of salt (optional)
¼ tsp mixed spice or cinnamon

1 Combine all ingredients in a medium saucepan. Bring to the boil, stirring frequently, then turn down heat and simmer for 5 minutes. Remove from heat and pour into bowls. Serve with non-dairy milk.

Microwave Method:
Combine ingredients and place in a microwave-safe bowl. Microwave on high for 1½ minutes, then stir. Cook a further minute. Continue to cook in 30-second bursts or until desired consistency is reached.

PER SERVE: *Energy 664 kJ (159 Cal); Protein 4g (9%); Carbohydrates 31g (84%); Sugars 18g; Fat 1g (7%); Fibre 5g; Sodium 6mg; Calcium 40mg.*

SERVES 2

Berry Couscous

1 cup uncooked couscous
2 cups orange juice (or other fruit juice)
1 cinnamon stick
2 tsp orange rind
1lb frozen berries of choice
7oz soy yoghurt

1 Place couscous in a mixing bowl. In a saucepan, combine juice, cinnamon stick and orange rind, and bring to the boil. Remove from heat and pour over couscous. Cover and leave for about 5 minutes, or until liquid is absorbed. Remove cinnamon stick. Separate the grains of couscous with a fork and gently add most of the berries.

2 Serve into bowls, sprinkling remaining berries over the top. Allow to stand for a few minutes to allow the berries to defrost, if desired.

3 Serve with yoghurt.

PER SERVE: Energy 1349 kJ (322 Cal); Protein 10g (12%); Carbohydrates 62g (80%); Sugars 26g; Fat 3g (8%); Fibre 4g; Sodium 23mg; Calcium 91mg.

SERVES 4

Berry Muffins

1½ cups all-purpose flour
½ cup sugar
1 tsp baking powder
1 tsp baking soda
¼ tsp salt
¾ cup non-dairy milk
⅓ cup oil
1 tsp vanilla extract
1 tsp cinnamon (optional)
1 cup frozen blueberries or
other berries

1 Preheat oven to 375°F and grease muffin tray.

2 In a large bowl, mix flour, baking powder, baking soda, cinnamon and salt. In another bowl, combine non-dairy milk, oil and vanilla extract. Add milk mixture and berries to the flour mixture, and gently stir with a fork until just combined.

3 Spoon mixture into muffin tray. Bake for 15–20 minutes or until a toothpick comes out clean.

4 Let the muffins sit in the tins for 10 minutes before cooling them on a wire cooling rack.

Variation: For chocolate chip muffins, use non-dairy chocolate chips in place of berries and cocoa in place of cinnamon.

PER SERVE: *Energy 1084 kJ (259 Cal); Protein 4g (6%); Carbohydrates 36g (57%); Sugars 16g; Fat 11g (37%); Fibre 2g; Sodium 338mg; Calcium 41mg.*

SERVES 8

Economical Muesli

5 cups rolled oats
1½ cups sunflower seeds
1½ cups coconut
¼ tsp salt
2 tbsp brown sugar (or honey)
2-3 tbsp oil
½–¾ cup fruit juice
1–2 cups dried fruit of your choice

1 Preheat oven to 210°F.

2 Combine rolled oats, sunflower seeds, coconut and salt in a large bowl. In a separate bowl, whisk brown sugar, oil and fruit juice. Mix through dry ingredients.

3 Place the mixture on a baking tray and cook for approximately 1 hour, stirring every 20 minutes.

4 When the muesli is toasted, mix in your choice of dried fruit. Turn oven off and leave muesli in oven until cold.

Variation: Add pumpkin seeds or any other muesli ingredients to taste.

PER SERVE: Energy 1771 kJ (423 Cal); Protein 11g (10%); Carbohydrates 43g (45%); Sugars 19g; Fat 21g (45%); Fibre 10g; Sodium 66mg; Calcium 80mg.

SERVES 10–12

Fresh Muesli

4 cups rolled oats
½ cup sultanas
½ cup coconut
15oz can crushed pineapple in
natural juice
1 apple, grated
3–4 cups apple juice

1 Mix rolled oats, sultanas and coconut. Add apple and pineapple, then mix well. Pour over apple juice until mixture is moist. Cover and refrigerate overnight.

2 Stir prior to serving. Serve with fruit and soy yoghurt.

PER SERVE: *Energy 1056 kJ (252 Cal); Protein 6g (9%); Carbohydrates 43g (74%); Sugars 23g; Fat 5g (17%); Fibre 6g; Sodium 18mg; Calcium 50mg.*

SERVES 8–10

Overnight Oatmeal

1 cup rolled oats
1 cup non-dairy milk
1 tbsp currants or raisins
½ tsp cinnamon

1 Combine all ingredients in a bowl and mix well. Cover and refrigerate overnight.

2 Enjoy the cereal cold the next morning or microwave until warmed. Stir in seasonal berries or other fruit, if desired.

PER SERVE: *Energy 2123 kJ (507 Cal); Protein 22g (17%); Carbohydrates 69g (59%); Sugars 10g; Fat 14g (24%); Fibre 11g; Sodium 117mg; Calcium 415mg.*

SERVES 1

1 cup rolled oats
¼ cup flaked almonds
¼ cup dried apricots, chopped
¼ cup dates or prunes, chopped
¼ cup shredded coconut
1 apple, grated
1 cup soy yoghurt
fruit juice or non-dairy milk to thin

Swiss Muesli

1 Combine all ingredients, cover and refrigerate for 2 hours (or overnight).
Suggestion: This muesli can be topped with sliced banana, strawberries or yoghurt.

PER SERVE: *Energy 1072 kJ (256 Cal); Protein 8g (13%); Carbohydrates 33g (57%); Sugars 20g; Fat 9g (30%); Fibre 6g; Sodium 14mg; Calcium 121mg.*

SERVES 4

2 cups cooked quinoa
½ cup light coconut cream
½ cup vanilla soy milk
1–2 tbsp honey

Creamed Quinoa

1 Mix all ingredients in a medium saucepan. Bring to the boil and reduce heat, allowing the mixture to thicken for about 15 minutes.

2 Cover and chill in the fridge for several hours.

Suggestion: Serve with fresh fruit and almonds.

PER SERVE: *Energy 1114 kJ (266 Cal); Protein 8g (12%); Carbohydrates 37g (61%); Sugars 10g; Fat 8g (27%); Fibre 6g; Sodium 32mg; Calcium 62mg.*

SERVES 4

Seven-Grain Cereal

¼ cup husked millet
¼ cup wholegrain rolled oats
¼ cup cracked wheat
¼ cup cracked rye
¼ cup buckwheat
¼ cup quinoa
¼ cup coarse corn meal
3½ cup water

1 Place grains and water in a medium saucepan on stove. Bring to the boil, then set stove as low as possible and simmer with the lid on for 12–15 minutes.

2 Turn stove off and leave until ready to eat.

PER SERVE: *Energy 737 kJ (176 Cal); Protein 6g (14%); Carbohydrates 32g (79%); Sugars 0.5g; Fat 1g (7%); Fibre 4g; Sodium 5mg; Calcium 21mg.*

SERVES 5

Five-Grain Cereal (Gluten-free)

amaranth
quinoa
brown rice
buckwheat
millet
water

1 Mix equal quantities of grains together. Mix 1 cup of grains with 2½ cups of water. Bring to the boil and simmer for 20–30 minutes.

Note: For both of these cereals, change the proportions of grains to taste. Try adding dried or fresh fruit.

Suggestions: Serve with fruit and soy milk, or make up a fruit smoothie and pour over the grains. Add nuts and raisins, if desired, or other pureed or chopped fruit.

PER SERVE: *Energy 682 kJ (163 Cal); Protein 5g (13%); Carbohydrates 31g (81%); Sugars 0.5g; Fat 2g (6%); Fibre 3g; Sodium 4mg; Calcium 14mg.*

Waffles

1 cup quick-cooking oats
½ cup oat bran
½ cup all-purpose flour
½ tsp baking powder
3 tbsp brown sugar
½ tsp ground cinnamon
¼ tsp ground nutmeg
¼ tsp salt
1¾ cup soy milk
2 tbsp margarine, melted (or bran oil)

1 Mix all ingredients together. Allow to sit for 5 minutes, then cook in half-cup measures in waffle iron until golden.

PER SERVE: *Energy 1394 kJ (333 Cal); Protein 11g (13%); Carbohydrates 44g (56%); Sugars 12g; Fat 5g (31%); Fibre 5g; Sodium 324mg; Calcium 190mg.*

SERVES 4

Almond Cream

¼ cup almond meal (process whole almonds until fine)
¼ cup hot water
¾ cup lite coconut cream
1 tbsp honey
½ tsp vanilla
1½ tbsp all-purpose flour

1 Whisk almond meal with hot water in a small saucepan. Add remaining ingredients and whisk until smooth. Stir constantly over medium heat until boiling and thickened. Cool, then refrigerate.

2 Blend with a little extra water or coconut milk if a thin cream is desired.

PER SERVE: *Energy 282 kJ (67 Cal); Protein 1g (6%); Carbohydrates 4g (23%); Sugars 3g; Fat 5g (71%); Fibre 1g; Sodium 5mg; Calcium 8mg.*

SERVES 10

1 cup currants
½ cup water
⅓ cup coconut

Coconut and Currant Spread

1 Place currants and water in a saucepan. Simmer on low heat for 15–20 minutes.

2 Transfer the mixture into a blender or food processor. Add coconut and process until evenly mixed and finely chopped.

PER SERVE: *Energy 272 kJ (65 Cal); Protein 1g (4%); Carbohydrates 10g (67%); Sugars 10g; Fat 2g (29%); Fibre 2g; Sodium 8mg; Calcium 14mg.*

SERVES 10

Strawberry Spread

1 cup dried pineapple pieces,
chopped
2 cups frozen strawberries

1 Place pineapple in a bowl with strawberries on top. Cover and leave several hours until pineapple has softened (overnight is good).

2 Blend in food processor until smooth.

3 Store covered in fridge for up to a week.

Variation: This spread can be made using a variety of fruits. For example, try replacing the frozen strawberries with frozen blueberries.

PER SERVE: *Energy 213 kJ (51 Cal); Protein 2g (13%); Carbohydrates 9g (85%); Sugars 9g; Fat 0.1g (2%); Fibre 3g; Sodium 4mg; Calcium 29mg.*

SERVES 10

5oz soft or silken tofu
1 banana (fresh or frozen)
½ tbsp brown sugar
1 cup fruit juice of choice
½ tsp vanilla extract (or
cinnamon if using apple juice)

Breakfast Shake

1 Place tofu and banana into a food processor or blender and process until smooth (about 1 minute). Add remaining ingredients and process until mixed.

PER SERVE: *Energy 770 kJ (184 Cal); Protein 7g (18%); Carbohydrates 29g (64%); Sugars 26g; Fat 4g (18%); Fibre 3g; Sodium 18mg; Calcium 97mg.*

SERVES 2

Hearty Fruit Smoothie

15oz can peaches or apricots in juice
1 banana, sliced
1½ cups non-dairy milk
2 tbsp passionfruit syrup
2 tbsp rolled oats
1 tbsp LSA*
½ tsp vanilla extract (optional)

1 Puree all the ingredients in a blender until smooth.

*LSA is equal quantities of linseed, almonds and sunflower seeds ground together.

PER SERVE: *Energy 1505 kJ (359 Cal); Protein 13g (14%); Carbohydrates 42g (51%); Sugars 30g; Fat 14g (35%); Fibre 7g; Sodium 95mg; Calcium 265mg.*

SERVES 2

Weights and measures

As the recipes in this book were developed and tested in New Zealand, the weights and measures are based on New Zealand metric standards. A standard measuring cup holds 250 millilitres; a tablespoon (tbsp) holds 15 millimetres (½ fl oz); and a teaspoon (tsp) is 5 millimetres (⅙ fl oz). United States standard measures of tablespoons and teaspoons are equivalent to these measures but a cup is a slightly smaller measure (about 240 millilitres or 8 fl oz), so use a generous cup.
The following conversion tables give only approximate equivalents but these variations should not affect cooking results.

Metric cup and spoon sizes

¼ cup = 2 fl oz	½ tsp = ¾ fl oz
⅓ cup = 3 fl oz	1 tsp = 1⅔ fl oz
½ cup = 4 fl oz	1 tbsp = ½ fl oz
1 cup = 8 fl oz	

Oven Temperatures

	°F (Fahrenheit)	°C (Celsius)
Very slow	250	120
Slow	275-300	150
Moderately slow	325	170
Moderate	350-375	180
Moderately hot	400	200
Hot	425-450	220
Very hot	475	240

Length
(imperial to metric)

⅛ in = 3 mm
¼ in = 6 mm
½ in = 1 cm
¾ in = 2 cm
1 in = 2.5 cm
2 in = 5 cm
2½ in = 6 cm
3 in = 8 cm
4 in = 10 cm
5 in = 13 cm
6 in = 15 cm
7 in = 18 cm
8 in = 20 cm
9 in = 23 cm
10 in = 25 cm
11 in = 28 cm
12 in (1 ft) = 30 cm

Weight
(imperial to metric)

1 oz = 30g
2 oz = 60g
3 oz = 90g
4 oz (¼lb) = 125g
5 oz = 155g
6 oz = 185g
7 oz = 220g
8 oz (½lb) = 250g
9 oz = 280g
10 oz = 315g
11 oz = 345g
12 oz (¾lb) = 375g
13 oz = 410g
14 oz = 440g
15 oz = 470g
16 oz (1lb) = 500g (0.5kg)
24 oz (1½lb) = 750g
32 oz (2lb) = 1000g (1kg)

Liquids
(metric cup to imperial to metric)

¼ cup = 2 fl oz = 60ml
½ cup = 4 fl oz = 125ml
¾ cup = 6 fl oz = 200ml
1 cup = 8 fl oz = 250ml
1¼ cups = 10 fl oz = 300ml
1½ cups = 12 fl oz = 375ml
1¾ cups = 14 fl oz = 425ml
2 cups = 16 fl oz = 500ml
2½ cups = 20 fl oz (1 pint) = 620ml

Glossary

allspice, also known as pimento or Jamaican pepper. Tastes like a blend of cinnamon, clove and nutmeg.

amaranth is a grain with high protein, high fibre and a nutty flavor.

baking soda, also known as bicarbonate of soda.

bok choy, also known as pak choi. An Asian green vegetable with a fresh, mild taste, often used in stir-fries.

buckwheat is a kind of grain that contains no gluten and is available from most health food stores.

bulgur wheat, a nutritious, high-fibre grain.

capsicum, also known as bell peppers or red peppers, is available in a range of colors, most commonly red, yellow and green.

chickpeas, also known as garbanzos. This legume is sandy-colored and irregularly round. May be purchased canned or in dried form for cooking at home.

cinnamon stick, dried inner bark from the cinnamon tree, used for flavoring but then discarded.

coconut cream, a cream made from pressing fresh coconut flesh. It is usually available in cans or cartons.

coriander, also known as cilantro or Chinese parsley, is a strongly-flavored herb added to a dish just before serving or as a garnish.

couscous, a fine, grain-like cereal product, is often used in Middle-Eastern and northern-African cooking.

curry powder is a blend of ground spices commercially available for ease of cooking. Can range from mild to hot.

eggplant, also known as aubergine.

filo pastry, tissue-thin pastry sheets that are usually prepared with oil or butter. This can be used for either savory or sweet dishes.

garam masala, a blend of spices often used in the cooking of northern India.

ginger, also known as green or root ginger. The root of the ginger plant is usually grated or finely chopped as a flavoring.

hummus, a dip or spread made primarily from chickpeas and sesame seeds.

Indian tomatoes are tomatoes canned with a selection of Indian herbs and spices.

Italian tomatoes are tomatoes canned with a selection of Italian herbs.

kumara, also known as sweet potato.

quinoa is a South-American grain with high protein and nutritional value, gluten-free.

roti, Indian flat bread.

spring onions, also known as scallions or shallots.

tofu is the curd from coagulated soy milk. Available in soft, silken and firm varieties, it is used for different purposes in cooking.

Udon noodles, from Japanese-style cooking, are a thick wheat-flour noodle.

yeast flakes, also known as nutritional yeast, yeshi or Brufax.

yellow mustard, also known as Ameria mustard or regular mustard. This mild mustard is bright yellow because of the turmeric among its ingredients.

"If people take charge of their lifestyle — especially how they eat — their healthy lifestyle will take care of them."

- Dr Hans Diehl

Recipe index

Acknowledgements

Project Manager and Recipe Collator: Rebekah Rankin

Project Director: Paul Rankin

Head Chef: Nola Presnall

Assistant Chef: Keryn McCutcheon

Recipe Tester: Sonia Rankin

Photography: Gary and Dyanne Dixon

Food Stylists: Nola Presnall, Keryn McCutcheon, Carolyn Atkinson, Dianne Cavaney, Gary and Dyanne Dixon

Recipe Contributors: Leonora Hurlow, Juleen and Allan Foote, Lorraine Curtis, Jeremy Dixon, Anne Anderson, Sibilla Johnson, Carolyn Atkinson, Keryn McCutcheon, Christchurch CHIP team, Russell and Laurel Wooley, Sarah Collins, Palmerston North CHIP team, Nola Presnall, Sonia Rankin, Rebekah Rankin